TRAIL OF PERFECTION

(Physical and Spiritual Trailblazer)

O.I. ONESIMUS

TRAIL OF PERFECTION
© 2023 O.I. Onesimus

Published by:
Rectify Mission Stardom
E-mail: ogunjobionesimus@gmail.com

ISBN: 978-978-792-805-9

All rights reserved.
No part of this book may be reproduced or transmitted in any form or by any means without the written permission of the author.

TABLE OF CONTENTS

FOREWORD

PREFACE

CHAPTER 1: SPIRITUAL INSIGHT

Spirit of Man
Holy Spirit
Evil Spirit(s)

CHAPTER 2: BIRD PERCH

Attribution
Possession

CHAPTER 3: SUPERNATURAL FORCES

Angels
Satan
Beast

CHAPTER 4: GREATER THAN ALL

Moses
Elijah
Solomon

CHAPTER 5: FATHER

Father Above
Father Within

CHAPTER 6: REAL WORD

Old Heaven and Earth
New Heaven and Earth

CHAPTER 7: SPIRITUAL WARFARE

At-a-Stretch (One)
At-a-Stretch (Two)
Armageddon

FOREWORD

Our Lord Jesus Christ came that he may preach about the Kingdom of God.
For he says in Matthew 4:17; "Repent, for the kingdom of heaven is at hand."

In these times, we have a unique opportunity of turning away from our sins so that we may be received into this kingdom by accepting the salvation which our Lord Jesus Christ has purchased with his blood and offered up to mankind. People of this world use their reason to sin i.e. they receive God's command but do not keep them; they accept the law and then disobey it, so what excuse can they hope to offer at judgment?

We realize that each one of us has an individual responsibility towards achieving this goal of salvation and we must therefore willingly submit ourselves to the will of the father just as the Son did after which he received Glory from the Father.
Psalm 49:13-15 says;

"This is the fate of those who have foolish confidence, the end of those who are pleased with their portion. Like sheep they are appointed for Sheol, Death shall be their shepherd; straight to the grave they descend, and their form shall waste away; Sheol shall be their home. But God will ransom my soul from the power of Sheol, for he will receive me."

My prayer for our dear beloved readers is that the Lord Almighty will draw us into Himself that we may receive the full prize of salvation and that his death and resurrection will not be in vain in our lives. Amen.

And so, we are to have the knowledge of Christ and hold on steadfast to what we have or know. We must press on to make this salvation our own just as Christ has made us His i.e. anyone that accepts Him.

We are to "Look to ourselves, that we may not lose what we have worked for, but may win the full reward."

For no one knows the time or the hour when the Lord Jesus Christ will return and so we must be willing to remain awake unto him, with extra oil at hand as the five wise virgins were unto the bridegroom according to Matthew 25:1-13, that we may be counted as wise ones on that great day.

Act 3:21 says;
"He must remain in Heaven until the time comes for all things to be made new, as God announced through his holy prophets who lived long ago."

We then must prepare ourselves so that He will transform our lowly bodies that they will be like His glorious body.

For without this new Glorious body, we would not be able to ascend into the new Jerusalem.

"Then I saw a new heaven and a new earth; for the first heaven and the first earth had passed away, and the sea was no more. And I saw the holy city, new Jerusalem, coming down out of heaven from God, prepared as a bride adorned for her husband; and I heard a loud voice from the throne saying, "Behold, the dwelling of God is with men. He will dwell with them, and they shall be his people, and God himself will be with them; he will wipe away every tear from their eyes, and death shall be no more, neither shall there be mourning nor crying nor pain any more, for the former things have passed away." - Revelation 21:1-4.

The second coming of Christ, would not be about further preaching of repentance or of the coming of the kingdom; for by then, the kingdom shall be made manifest.

Whereas, His own flock, who received the message of the Kingdom, God will receive them and the Kingdom of God will be theirs.

Let us then endeavor to keep careful watch to the end for the word says, "But when a righteous man turns away from his righteousness and commits iniquity, and does according to all the abominations that the wicked man does, shall he live? All the righteousness which he has done shall not be remembered; because of the unfaithfulness of which he is guilty and the sin which he has committed, because of them he shall die." - Ezekiel 18:24.

May our faithfulness unto Him be as brides worthy of the title; "THE LAMB'S BRIDE."
This book, that is divinely written by its author, will look to direct our ways and realign our steps, so that we can be helped by the Holy Spirit that He may lead us to the Father and remain firmly fixed in Him in order that our lowly bodies may be resurrected and ascended into Glory with the Lord and Savior, Jesus Christ. Amen.

Apostle E.O. Aniamalu

PREFACE

Man is beyond a spirit being. Literarily, a living man is comprised of a body, soul and spirit (Thessalonians 5:23).

Man, in this book, represents both male and female (Genesis 5:2) except if specifically stated to mean male.

The emphasis in this book is basically on man's spirit, in view of God's word which is infallible.

In other words, TRAIL OF PERFECTION is not of mental accent, theoretical or theological work but of absolute revelation by God's word through the HOLY SPIRIT.

This is not just a book but a divine message to this '21st Century' era or dispensation and more to come if Jesus Christ tarries.
The bold sentences in this book are scriptural quotations however, the scriptural tags in bracket, are references to the divine write-up.

Therefore, you are honorably enjoined to follow the book in order of its content.

May GOD bless you even as you read on.

CHAPTER 1: SPIRITUAL INSIGHT

Spirit of Man

The spirit of man is the candle of the LORD, searching all the inward parts of the belly – Proverbs 20: 27 KJV.

GOD by Himself breathed into the dust that He had mold (Genesis 2:7) as He said that let us make man in Our image, after our likeness (Genesis 1:26-27).

Adam was known to be that man (Genesis 2:19-20). Therefore, the (seen) dust that ever lived, living and that would ever live if Christ tarries, was channeled through the man Adam (Romans 5:12-14, Genesis 3:20) in a particular order, chain or line often referred to as lineage (Genesis chapter 5, 1 Chronicles chapter 1 – chapter 9, Matthew chapter 1).

Now unto the King eternal, immortal, invisible, the only wise GOD, be honor and glory forever and ever. Amen. – 1 Timothy 1: 17 KJV.

He (GOD) created all things, both visible (seen) and invisible (unseen) things through His Word (John 1 :1 – 3).

The spirit of man is not the only unseen part of man but GOD uses the spirit of man to search all other unseen or inward parts of that man; normally referred to as heart (mind) or belly according to King James Version.

The body is the physical part (seen) of a man as this Earth is also physical in nature. The body is comprised of the head, hand, heart etc.

On the other hand, the spiritual part of a man has attributes as the physical part according to the scriptures (Genesis 1:26-27, Ephesians 3:16-17, Acts 28:25-27, 1 Peter 3:4) but it is unseen in nature just as Heaven is unseen (Hebrews 4:12-13).

There are divers Theological, Philosophical and Mythological explanation of a man's soul but in reality, Holy Bible, has it that the body, soul and spirit are the whole of a man (human being) (1 Thessalonians 5:23, Hebrews 4:12-13, Daniel 7:15) despite the similarities and differences in nature of the three entities.

The body, soul and spirit have to be together for a man to be a living being (Genesis 2:7, Luke 8:54-55).

The body, soul and spirit of a man are important to GOD however, the spirit of man is the area of focus in this book and Jesus Christ is the case study.

Spirit generally, is one of the divine natures (2 Peter 1:2-4, Genesis 1:26-27).

Jesus Christ as a man even when on Earth, and as a son of man, has his human spirit (1 John 4:3, John 1: 14-34, John 8:54, Luke 23:46) since every man have a body, soul and spirit.

Jesus Christ said to His disciples that the words He speaks, are spirit and life.

Well, only Jesus Christ is termed as life (John 14:6) nevertheless, any other person may have life (Jesus Christ).

Every person however, have his or her own 'spirit man' (1 Corinthians 5:3-4, 1 Corinthians 2:11).
Every word spoken into a man is of great significance to that man (Matthew 12:36-37).

Whether a man speaks outwardly or not, there is constantly an ongoing word(s) reading inside of him as long as he is alive.

Once a man is activated in the spiritual realm from birth, he is either nurtured by words of life or the opposite of that, from the surrounding realm. Nevertheless, the man (male or female) exist a default being.

God anointed Jesus the Christ with the Holy Spirit and with power (Acts 10:38). In other words, it shows clearly that right from birth, Jesus was nurtured by the Holy Spirit.

He had people (friends, neighbors, siblings, mother and 'father') who had always conversed with him and of which that was fine but in all spoken words to him or around him, the Holy Spirit utterly nurtured his spirit (John 7:2-10, Matthew 12:46-50).

For every human being, it is expedient that his spirit is either nurtured out rightly by the Holy Spirit or by Evil spirit(s) even before birth.

Despite the breath of life in man since creation, man is free-willed (Genesis 2:16-17, Joshua 24:15, John 7:17, Proverbs 16:9, Revelation 3:20) and GOD remains GOD forever. Amen.

The passages; Romans 3:23, Genesis 3:1-19 and Romans 5:12 – makes known that at a point in time from creation, man fell off the standard or glory of GOD, and ever since then, the expedient nature of man to be nurtured by the Holy Spirit, left no other option but for evil spirit(s) to be attached to him and to nurture him because of the fell-off.

Therefore, all men are bound right from conception, to be nurtured by evil spirit(s).
GOD, in His infinite wisdom, made a way out for man unto anyone that willingly accepts Him (John 14:6, Hebrews 1:1-3, John 3:16).

True prophets spoke but in part(s); Jesus Christ is the complete word of GOD to man for life (1 Corinthians 13:8-10, Matthew 5:17) and it is through every (complete) word of GOD that any man can make-it up with GOD (Matthew 4:4).

You may pause at this moment to examine yourself in the light of the scripture before you proceed in the study.

God bless you!

Holy Spirit

For there are three that bear record in heaven, the Father, the Word, and the Holy Ghost: and these three are one – 1 John 5:7 KJV

If a man is saved, the spirit of that man is changed by God through Christ Jesus (2 Corinthians 3:16, John 3:6, Ephesians 4:21-24).

Therefore, if any man be in Christ, he is a new creature: old things are passed away; behold all things are become new – 2 Corinthians 5:17 KJV.

The saved man then needs to be utterly nurtured by the Holy Spirit so as to be receptive to Christ; even to GOD and his kingdom (Matthew 3:11, Romans 8:16).

Jesus answered and said unto him, verily, verily, I say unto thee, except a man be born again, he cannot see the kingdom of GOD – John 3:3 KJV.

Jesus answered, verily, verily, I say unto thee, except a man be born of water and of the spirit, he cannot enter into the kingdom of GOD – John 3:5 KJV.

Anywhere or place that a saved man finds himself, divers' word is spoken around him. GOD has to release the Holy spirit upon and into that spirit of man as an attachment to him by Christ Jesus (John 14:16-17).

Only GOD can do this release of the Holy Spirit into any man as he did to Jesus His Son (Acts 10:38, Acts 15:8-9).

Nevertheless, a saved man could ask of GOD for that release of the Holy Spirit by Christ Jesus (Luke 11:13).

Holy Spirit is one with Jesus Christ (Word) and with the Father (Most High). They say and mean same.

Jesus says – I have yet many things to say unto you, but ye cannot bear them now. Howbeit when he, the spirit of truth, is come, he will guide you into all truth: for he shall not speak of himself; but whatsoever he shall hear, that shall he speak: and he will show you things to come. He shall glorify me: for he shall receive of mine, shall show it unto you. All things that the Father hath are mine: therefore, said I that he shall take of mine, and shall show it unto you – John 16:12-15.

Upon a man that does not accept Jesus Christ, the Holy Spirit convict such of his sins but the Holy Spirit (Spirit of holiness) is not one with unclean or evil spirit(s) (John 16:7-11, Acts 2:38-47).

"Anyone who speak a word against the son of man, it will be forgiven him; but whoever speaks against the Holy Spirit, it will not be forgiven him, either in this age or in the age to come – Matthew 12:32 NKJV.

The Holy Spirit convict sinners of their sins and if any of such heed not as to repent, such a one shall surely face the consequence of his unrepentance but if such a one hearkens to the conviction of the Holy Spirit by turning to the Father (Most High One) through Jesus Christ (His Son) for forgiveness, then shall he be saved from eternal destruction.

To a child of GOD, the Holy Spirit bears witness with such a one even towards bearing fruit of the Spirit and such would receive the reward, benefit and be more grown except if he hearkens not.

Anti-Christ and even false prophets understand the convictions of the Holy Spirit in the spiritual realm but they resist (blaspheme) him directly or indirectly because of their fleshy desires (John 16:8-11).

Jesus Christ (Word of GOD) is given to all. All that accepts him have the common faith in GOD. Nevertheless, the language of the Holy Spirit to every individual may differ despite the common message. Also, the All-knowing GOD has His voice to every soul, for GOD is Love (Titus 1:4, Matthew 24:14, 1 John 4:8- 9).

"While peter yet spake these words, the Holy Ghost fell on all them which heard – Acts 10:44 NKJV.

The language of GOD to Prophet Isaiah (Isaiah 9:6) was different from that to Prophet Jeremiah (Jeremiah 23:5- 6); the language of GOD to Apostle Peter was different from that to Apostle Paul (Galatians 2:8).

In other words, despite the different languages or tongues to everyone (spirit being) from above, the Word of GOD remains same to all; the words of Christ Jesus are spirit and they are life.

For example, if Jesus Christ says that a man (male or female) should not have more than one spouse (Genesis 5:2); what justification does any man have to divorce or go contrary to the saying according to Mark 10:6-12, irrespective of his title before GOD?

Is there any diplomacy in GOD's Word?

Why should men debate GOD's Word rather than simply obey His Word that is forever settled in Heaven (Psalms 119:89)?

Even if a man or woman that is known by GOD, separates from his spouse for the sake of fornication (GOD forbid!).
As long as that his spouse still has the breath of life, the man or woman is not to re-marry no matter the physical or spiritual distance that may be between them. (1 Corinthians 7:1-11, Matthew 5:27-32, Matthew 19:3-11, 1 Peter 3:1-9, Malachi 2:11-16, Romans 7:2-3, Hebrews 13:4).

If it pleases the man or woman, his spouse may be reconciled to him afterwards or the separation does not even occur in the first place as he/she may choose [Great eternal mystery] (Ephesians 5:15-33).

But he answered and said, "It is written, 'man shall not live by bread alone, but by every word that proceeds from the mouth of GOD.'" - Matthew 4:4 NKJV.

What is the Almighty GOD saying to you in this book according to His word, if you accept his word?

Jesus Christ worked and walked absolutely by the power of the Holy Spirit even when he was on Earth. He always detached the spirit of men from their attachment to evil spirits since he himself is the word of GOD and the Holy Spirit is one with him (Isaiah 66:16, Matthew 3:11, Ephesians 6:17-18, Matthew 12:28).

Jesus Christ never killed any man when he was on Earth. Note that Jesus Christ detached evil spirits from man (James 4:7) but he did not commit any murder case as to detach the spirit of man from man (Matthew 5:38-39, James 4:11-12, Matthew 5:43-45).

Jesus says – Ye have heard that it was said by they of old time, thou shalt not kill, and whosoever shall kill shall be in danger of the judgment: But I say unto you, that whosoever is angry with his brother without a cause shall be in danger of the judgment: and whosoever shall say to his brother, Raca, shall be in danger of the council: but whosoever shall say, thou fool, shall be in danger of hell fire – Matthew 5:21-22 KJV.

In salvation; the spirit of man is changed by GOD and unto GOD. More so in deliverance, the spirit of man is being detached from its attachment to evil spirits by GOD. In sanctification, which is on the same page as deliverance; the spirit of man is being nurtured by the Holy Spirit (Isaiah 66:16, 1 Corinthians 6:17).

You may pause at this moment to examine yourself in the baptism of the Holy Spirit.

GOD bless you!

Evil Spirit(s)

Evil spirit (d'evil) is the opposite of Holy Spirit even over a man (Romans 8:9, Galatians 5:19-23, Acts 13:43-45).

Man cannot fight against evil spirit(s) by his own spirit. Only the Holy Spirit can be against evil spirit(s) of which the spirit of man that is attached to evil spirit is also endangered during the fight except if saved (Matthew 12:43-45, Acts 5:1-11).

So shall they fear the name of the Lord from the west, and his glory from the rising of the sun. When the enemy shall come in like a flood the spirit of the Lord shall lift up a standard against him – Isaiah 59:19 KJV.

Evil spirit(s) goes out and bow to the name of Jesus Christ, even to his authority (Acts 16:18, I Corinthians 8:4-6, Hebrews 4:12). Man can only fight against evil spirit(s) by the Holy Spirit.

For as many as are led by the Spirit of GOD, they are the sons of GOD – Romans 8:14 KJV.

Redeeming the time, because the days are evil – Ephesians 5:16 NKJV.

Blessed is the man to whom the LORD does not impute iniquity, and in whose spirit, there is no deceit – Psalms 32:2 NKJV.

Do not be overcome by evil, but overcome evil with good – Romans 12:21 NKJV.

"Watch and pray, lest you enter into temptation. The spirit indeed is willing but the flesh is weak". – Matthew 26:41 NKJV.

CHAPTER 2: BIRD PERCH

Attribution

And John bore witness, saying, "I saw the Spirit descending from heaven like a dove, and he remained upon Him. "I did not know Him, but he who sent me to baptize with water said to me, 'upon whom you see the spirit descending, and remaining on Him; this is he who baptizes with the Holy Spirit.' "And I have seen and testified that this is the Son of GOD." – John 1:32-34 NKJV.

When he had been baptized, Jesus came up immediately from the water; and behold, the heavens were opened to him, and he saw the Spirit of GOD descending like a dove and alighting upon him. – Matthew 3:16 NKJV.

In the physical world or realm, different types of birds fly in the sky at different times over the head of a man that is programmed to be upon the face of the Earth. These birds could be vulture, dove, sparrow even eagle. It is also possible for instance, that a dove flying over a man perches or rest on the shoulder of that man. Some other birds such as parrot, sparrow, could as well perch on a man if they are permitted by him. Normally, birds of the same feathers fly together and so a parrot and dove may not possibly perch on a man at the same time, that is even if the man permits any of the birds to perch on him.

In the same vein, different types of spirit may fly at different times over any man (spirit being) in the spiritual world or realm (Revelation 19:17).
These spirits could be diver's kind of evil spirit, diver's kind of other human spirits or even the Holy Spirit. Nevertheless, a man is free-willed to permit any of these spirits to perch, rest or be attached to his own spirit.

Since birds of the same feathers fly together, it is not possible for the Holy Spirit to fly over an individual and for evil spirits to fly over the same individual simultaneously.

The Holy Spirit is far above all things (John 14:26, Isaiah 55:8-9).

As a dove has gentle and good attribute(s) unlike other birds, so also the Holy Spirit is attributed as the spirit of truth (John 16:13), spirit of holiness (Romans 1:4), spirit of wisdom (Isaiah 11:1-2) ... spirit of judgment (Isaiah 4:4).

Therefore, the Holy Spirit or the spirit of man that is attached to the Holy Spirit is known by the fruit they bear, according to Galatians 5:22-23. Also, Matthew 7:15-27.

Possession

It is not a crime for divers' kind of spirit to fly over man as a spirit (i.e. temptation is no crime) but man as a spirit being, could avoid temptations or unclean spirits from flying over him by the grace of GOD.

It is a crime however for man to permit or allow the perch of evil spirit(s) in him. The Holy Spirit descended like a dove and remained upon Jesus Christ and that should also be the testimony of the children of GOD (Acts chapter 2).

Evil spirit possesses or perches on any man that is not a child of GOD and they are predominantly upon him of which that is a crime, even an eternal crime.

Therefore, a child of GOD is mandated to test all spirits as to know by grace, which spirit(s) to permit upon or into himself and which one(s) that are not permitted (1 John 4:1, Acts 16:14-18). The unseen nature of the spiritual realm calls for discernment by children of the Most High GOD (1 Corinthians 2:16, Hebrews 5:13-14, 1 John 4:1-6).

These are days where GOD pours out his Spirit upon all flesh (Joel 2:28) so therefore, even the Holy Spirit is now and can fly in the spiritual realm over any man whether saved or unsaved but the flight of Holy Spirit over the unsaved ones is to convict them and not to baptize or perch on them. He could only perch or rest on a child of GOD, even towards eternity.

It is one thing for any spirit to fly over any man scripturally; it is another thing for a spirit to perch or reside in a man.

Therefore, despite the different spirits that may fly over or despite the diver's thoughts or temptation that may come to a child of GOD, and even despite the divers re- sounding voices just as Jesus Christ experienced immediately after Holy Spirit remained upon him (Matthew 4:1-11), it is only the Holy Spirit that prevails in his life.

The power of GOD makes that possible in the life of His children (1 John 5:4, 1 John 5:18). The Power of GOD can fall upon both animate and inanimate object (Acts 19:11-12). Yet again, it is possible for a child of GOD to always avoid the flight of evil spirit(s) or temptation over or in him by the indwelling of the Holy Spirit more and more in his life.
Holy Spirit is the possession of the children of GOD (Ephesians 1:9-14).

Then Jesus said to him, "Away with you, Satan!! For it is written, 'You shall worship the Lord your GOD and Him only you shall serve.'" Then the devil left Him, and behold, angels came and ministered to him. – Matthew 4:10-11 NKJV.

A life of praise, worship and service to GOD is attainable. The kingdom of God is void of evil and of which praise and worship unto GOD (Father, Son, Holy Spirit) never ceases in heaven (2 Chronicles 5:13-14, Revelation chapter 4, Revelation chapter 19).

You may kindly pause at the moment to examine the acknowledgement of GOD in your life.

GOD bless you!

CHAPTER 3: SUPERNATURAL FORCES

Angels

And of the angels he says: "Who makes His angels spirits and his ministers a flame of fire".
– Hebrews 1:7 NKJV, also Psalms 104:4.

Angels could be able to manifest in the natural realm as well as in the supernatural realm according to their endowment and empowerment by GOD. (Daniel 9:20- 22, Matthew 18:10, Luke 6:22).

God sends angel(s) to aid men especially His children (Hebrews 1:14, Hebrews 2:6-8, Hebrews 2:16).

Man may or may not fully understand angels on Earth (1 Corinthians 2:11-16) but at the end of all things, children of GOD shall be like angels (Matthew 22:30).

Angels are not to be worshipped however (Revelation 22:9).

Let no one cheat you of your reward, taking delight in false humility and worship of angels, intruding into those things which he has not seen, vainly puffed up by his fleshy mind – Colossians 2:18 NKJV.

Angles rejoices over a sinner that repent (Luke 15:10).

Satan

Satan is a fallen angel (Revelation 12:7-9, Isaiah 14:12-15, Ezekiel 28:6-8, Luke 10:18-20, Daniel 10:13).

GOD put enmity between man and Satan because he cast down Satan to the Earth yet created He man upon the Earth; He surrounds His saints with is hedge of which they are mandated to break not the hedge so as to sustain that enmity with Satan as well as maintain the angelic hedge (Genesis chapter 3, Revelation chapter12, Psalms 34:7, Ecclesiastes 10:8).

Satan as an entity that he is was not known in the realm of man until in the days of Job, despite the fact that he had always been before then.

Satan typified as Leviathan in Job 41:1 and as the serpent of old in Revelation 12:9, was in detail made known to man in the generation of Job (Job chapter 41). The All- Knowing One, made him known to man (Job chapter 38, 39 and chapter 40).

Men before the days of Job had always thought that GOD was responsible for the calamity or evil that befalls them (Deuteronomy chapter 27 and chapter 28). Some men knew that GOD does not do evil but were ignorant of the entity behind evil.

Madam Eve knew that a serpent deceived her but she did not know what the serpent really was (Genesis 3:13).

King David in his generation knew that he had human enemies but he did not fully understand the unseen or spiritual enemy (Psalms chapter 5).

Who can question or contend with GOD about all His creation?

Moreover, the LORD answered Job, and said: "shall the one who contends with the Almighty correct him? He who rebukes God, let him answer it." Then Job answered the LORD and said: "behold, I am vile; what shall I answer you? I lay my hand over my mouth. Once I have spoken, but I will not answer; yes, twice, but I will proceed no further."
Then the LORD answered Job out of the whirl wind, and said: "now prepare yourself like a man," I will question you, and you shall answer me: "would you indeed annul my judgment? Would you condemn me that you may be justified?
Have you an arm like GOD? Or can you thunder with a voice like his? – Job 40:1-9 NKJV.

At first, Job was confused about GOD's judgment because of his ignorance of what the Almighty GOD was showing to men through his own life.

Despite the confusion of Job, GOD exposed Satan even while Satan himself thought he had opportunity to do his worst to Job (Job 1:6-12).

For GOD is not the author of confusion but of peace, as in all churches of the saints – 1 Corinthians 14:33 KJV.

GOD later exposed, disgraced and destroyed the works of Satan in the presence of men through Jesus, the Christ.

He who sins is of the devil, for the devil has sinned from the beginning. For this purpose, the son of GOD was manifested, that He might destroy the works of the devil – 1 John 3:8 NKJV.

GOD is above all things (Zechariah 4:10b, Psalms 32:8) nevertheless, GOD does not do evil.

Satan does evil (Job 1:7, John 8:43-44). GOD is good (Mark 10:18, 1 John 1:5). Jesus as a man is good because of GOD (John 13:13-17).

In other words, from old times, men fell-off GOD's glory; men (willfully and/or ignorantly) drifted away from His goodness, holiness, blessings, love, light, unto darkness and dark kingdom (John 3:19).

THANK GOD!

Jesus, the Christ came to reconcile the same men back to GOD (Revelation 5:5, Isaiah chapter 53, John 3:16, Revelation 5).

Jesus Christ conquered Satan (Genesis 3:15, Hebrews 2:14-15, Colossians 2:15, 1 John 3:8).

Man's fight against Satan who is an opposition to the things of GOD, is not carnal (Zechariah 3:1-2, Revelation 12:10-11, 1 Peter 5:8-9, Matthew 16:22-23).

For the weapons of our warfare are not carnal but mighty in GOD for pulling down strong holds, casting down arguments and every high thing that exalt itself against the knowledge of GOD, bringing every thought into captivity to the obedience of Christ. – 2 Corinthians 10:4-5 NKJV.

Men practice diver's kind of rituals and religion in their attempt to reach GOD while neglecting the word of GOD to their situation.

Men cry, rant and pant instead of compliance with God's word (Jesus Christ) so as to cast out devils and utterly fight curses, calamity, failure, infirmities, lack and even the gates of hell (Matthew 16:15-19, Jeremiah 44:15:19).

GOD IS MERCIFUL (Ps 103:8)

GOD IS GRACIOUS (Ps 103:8)

GOD IS WONDERFUL (Isa 9:6)

GOD IS AWESOME (Ps 68:35, Ps 47:2)

GOD IS HOLY (1 Sam 2:2)

GOD IS WITH US (Matt 1:23)

GOD IS NOT MOCKED (Gal 6:7)

GOD IS POWERFUL (1 Chron 29:11)

GOD IS PERFECT (Matt 5:48)

GOD IS WORTHY TO BE PRAISED (Ps 145)

GOD IS FAITHFUL (1 Cor 1:9)

GOD IS GOOD (Ps 100:5)

GOD IS ABLE (2 Cor 9:8)

GOD LOVES YOU (Jn 3:16, Jn 15:12, Jer 29:11).

Now when all things are made subject to Him, then the Son Himself will also be subject to Him who put all things under Him, that GOD may be all in all. – 1 Corinthians 15:28 NKJV.

Chapter Seven of this book, says more into spiritual warfare.

Beast

Holy Bible tells that anti-Christ is not after rapture (return of Jesus) but before, for Jesus cometh only twice to this world for all people and not thrice (Isaiah 11:11). Therefore, you may brace- up.

The notion that there would still be people in Earth to suffer '666' era after rapture (i.e. after second coming of Jesus), is unscriptural.

This world ends at the second coming of Christ Jesus. The era '666' according to Revelation 13:18 is a relational expression of the terror and suffering from darkness/evil beast such as had never been, before Christ Jesus returns.

It would be as though everything is been corrupted by the evil beast and as though GOD and His angels rarely exist which is now being witnessed (Armageddon) but nay, there are still saints (remnant of Israel) (Romans 11:2-5); there are still those that are worshipping GOD in truth and in spirit. Only that they are few (Matthew 11:11-13, Romans 11:2-6).

All trials, persecution, perils, pestilence (works of the evil beast and anti-Christ) only last until Christ Jesus returns i.e. the second coming of Jesus.

It may be tempting to think that scripture infers that the second coming of Jesus is first and then after a thousand 'literal' years, cometh judgment day where everyone would array one after another BUT what scripture says is 'true'; there would be 'judgment day' nevertheless, GOD has committed all that into the hands of his Son (Jesus Christ) (John 5:22, Matthew 13:30, Matthew 25:31-46) who would do the filtering (separation) as to receive some, up into the sky and unto GOD forever while others together with Satan, to depart away into the lake of fire with their beast and anti-Christ inclusive (2 Thessalonians 2:3-12, Matthew chapter 25).

Evil Beast is like a robot, controlled by Satan. A robot may seem bigger and stronger that its controller but the controller is still the source of its operation(s).

(See Daniel chapter 7, Revelation chapter 13, Revelation 9:11, Revelation 11:7, Matthew chapter 25, 2 Thessalonians 2:9-10, Matthew 7:15, Revelation chapter 17, Titus 1:10-12, Philippians 3:18-19, 1 Thessalonians

4:15-18, 1 Thessalonians 5:1-2, 2 Thessalonians 1:6-8, Hebrews 9:28).

CHAPTER 4: GREATER THAN ALL

Moses

Miracle happened in the time of Moses despite that the sea parted (Exodus 13:17-22, also Exodus chapter 14); it was still logical for a man to walk on dry land but Jesus walked on water (Matthew 14:22-27) which is not logical.

The earth is the LORD's and the fullness thereof; the world, and they that dwell therein. For he hath founded it upon the seas, and established it upon the floods – Psalms 24:1-2 KJV.

This message is not to incite men as to start walking on water but this message is to strengthen towards standing strong in Jesus Christ despite the stormy sea and turbulent times.

The disciple is not above his master: but everyone that is perfect shall be as his master – Luke 6:40 KJV also Luke 4:4.

A day cometh where there shall be nothing impossible for a man that is in Christ Jesus. Jesus is the pilot whether or not his followers understand all the mysteries of spiritual endeavors' in life. Jesus is the pilot of both babes and maturing ones that are in him (1 Corinthians 13:11).

In other words, whether faith like a mustard seed (Matthew 17:20-21a) or faith bigger than the world itself (Acts 10:38 also Hebrews 11:1-2), would be made whole on that final day in the New Heaven and New Earth (Revelation 21:1-4) after this one is passed away (only for those who believe in Christ Jesus) (Matthew 24:35).

A day when all human and devilish words shall be swallowed up by the words of Jesus Christ and only his word shall be, just as the rod of Moses swallowed all other rods of Pharaoh (Exodus 7:10-12).

Moses was an embodiment of the law (John 7:19a, John 1:17).

Jesus Christ is greater that Moses.

Elijah

Miracle happened in the time of Elijah despite that chariot of fire had to take him alive (2 Kings 2:11) but Jesus ascended together with heavenly host into heaven, majestically (Luke 24:50-53, 1 Chronicles 16:27 also Mark 16:19).

And no man hath ascended up to heaven, but he that came down from heaven, even the Son of man which is in heaven – John 3:13 KJV also, Ephesians 4:10.

This message is to strengthen towards patiently awaiting the second coming of the LORD Jesus Christ (Mark 13:32-33) no matter how long it may take; whether some men be alive or sleep (John 11:25-26).

And this is the will of him that sent me, that everyone which seeth the son, and believeth on him, may have everlasting life: and I will raise him up at the last day – John 6:40 KJV.

In whom ye also trusted, after that ye heard the word of truth, the gospel of your salvation: in whom also after that ye believed, ye were sealed with that Holy Spirit of promise, which is the earnest of our inheritance until the redemption of the purchased possession, unto the praise of his glory – Ephesians 1:13-14 KJV.

Moses and Elijah as personalities, appeared to Jesus Christ on the mount of transfiguration when the son of man was to be glorified (Matthew 17:1-13).

Elijah was an embodiment of restoration (Mark 9:12 also Matthew 17:11, Luke 1:13-17).

Jesus Christ is greater than Elijah.

Solomon

Jesus supplied sufficient fish for the multitude from two fishes (Matthew 14:13-21). Does it show that he is a waster, knowing fully well that there are fishes in the market or in the ocean that may have been supplied instead?

GOD does not share his glory with anyone or thing despite that He created all things; if anyone becomes polluted, He can always give better one without transfer of the first or preceding creation into the other (i.e. they ate special/heavenly fish) (Isaiah 42:6-9).

Even as touching the second coming of Christ, those in Jesus and Jesus in them would be saved from the pollution of this world into another (best) world without the transfer of this present world's resources such as its oil and gas, gold, silver, into the new one, as this present world would then be passed away together with the corruptible body (Earth) of those alive and them that sleep, at the appearing of Jesus Christ in the air (John 14:1-3, John 15:4-7).

This message is not to avoid the purchase of fish in the market or being a fisherman but it is to strengthen towards the 'unlimited riches' of GOD now and forever (John 21:1-25, John 6:25-29, Philippians 4:19-20, Ephesians 4:28, 3 John 1:2).

"The queen of the south will rise up in the judgment with this generation and condemn it, for she came from the ends of the earth to hear the wisdom of Solomon; and indeed, a greater than Solomon is here – Matthew 12:42 NKJV.

Dear Reader,

The Lord has laid it in the heart of the writer of this book to publish several copies of it. This is for the gospel of Jesus Christ to reach the unreached ones, even in their various languages all over the world. Therefore, please leave your honest review and kindly give a high rating of this publication on the site of purchase to achieve this aim.

If you willingly want to support this ministry/project, kindly reach out via email on: ogunjobionesimus@gmail.com

God bless you!

Disclaimer: Please be informed that you could reach the writer through the above contact information above only. Kindly discard any other form of contact if encountered.

Thank you!

CHAPTER 5: FATHER

Father Above

At some points, Jesus Christ looked up towards Heaven as he addresses his Father while praying.

Then he commanded the multitudes to sit down on the grass. And he took the five loaves and the two fishes, and looking up to heaven, he blessed and broke and gave the loaves to the disciples; and the disciples gave to the multitudes – Matthew 14:19 NKJV.

If astronomers and/or astrologers (as human beings), travel trillion of trillion miles in space; even if they successfully get to the core of this present sun, they would never find the Creator (GOD) there (Hebrews 11:3).

Wherever GOD dwells, He is unseen to the manly realm.

Who above has immortality, dwelling in unapproachable light, whom no man has seen or can see, to whom be honor and everlasting power. Amen – 1 Timothy 6:16 NKJV.

GOD the Father, Son and Holy Spirit are one (1 John 5:7). Only Jesus the Christ is the Son of GOD and Jesus Christ is GOD [Great mystery] (John 1:1, Philippians 2:6-8).

All other children of GOD are adopted sons and daughters of GOD (Ephesians 1:5), through Christ Jesus (John 15:4-5).

Anyone that is properly disciplined by him, can be as him (Jesus) (Luke 6:40) but no other man or woman is Christ Jesus (Messiah) (Matthew 24:5, Matthew 1:18-25).

Jesus always use earthly narrations to describe the heavenly abode and to buttress GOD's kingdom (Matthew 20:1-16).

Therefore, the approach of a man (body, soul and spirit) towards GOD should be that of absolute thanksgiving, praises and worship unto Him.

Men may render honor to themselves (Romans 13:7) but worship only GOD (Acts 10:25-26).

"God is Spirit, and those who worship Him must worship in spirit and truth" – John 4:24 NKJV.

Father Within

At some points, Jesus Christ went on his knees, with his head lowered as he addresses his Father while praying.

He went a little farther and fell on his face, and prayed, saying, "O my father, if it is possible, let this cup pass from me; nevertheless, not as I will, but as you will." - Matthew 26:39 NKJV.

Wherever GOD dwells, He is unseen to the manly realm nevertheless, He is shown abroad through the Holy Spirit in any man that accepts Jesus Christ as his Lord and Savior (Matthew 16:16-18, Romans 10:13).

In other words, the Holy Spirit attached to the spirit of man, reveals Jesus Christ and Jesus Christ reveals the Father, even His counsel to that man (John 5:20, Luke 17:20-21, Romans 5:5-6).

Jesus said to him, "Have I been with you so long, and yet you have not known Me, Philip? He who has seen Me has seen the Father; so how can you say, 'show us the Father'?

"Do you not believe that I am in the Father, and the Father in Me? The words that I speak to you I do not speak on My own authority; but the Father who dwells in Me does the works. "Believe Me that I am in the Father and the Father in Me, or else believe Me for the sake of the works themselves. "Most assuredly, I say to you, he who believes in Me, the works that I do he will do also; and greater works than these he will do, because I go to My Father. "And whatever you ask in My name, that I will do, that the Father may be glorified in the Son. "If you ask anything in My name, I will do it. "If you love Me, keep My commandments. "And I will pray the father, and He will give you another Helper, that He may abide with you forever – the Spirit of truth, whom the world cannot receive, because it neither sees Him nor knows Him; but you know Him, for He dwells with you and will be in you. – John 14:9-17 NKJV.

A king is king over everyone in his kingdom, be it strangers, slaves, servants and even his sons. Nevertheless, the children of that king have the right to address him as father.

GOD is GOD; He is king over all His creation, even over all people but only His children can acceptably and eternally access Him as Father (John 1:12, 2 Corinthians 6:17-18).

Everlasting wrath only await unsaved ones.

GOD created all things for His good pleasure (Revelation 4:11).

GOD is everywhere even in Hell (Psalms 139:8, Proverbs 15:3) however, He is been called as "the GOD of heaven and the GOD of the earth" (Genesis 24:3, 1 Corinthians 8:5- 6).

For instance, GOD created everyone which includes Abraham, Nahor and Haran (Genesis 11:26-27, Galatians 3:16) however, He chooses to be called as "the GOD of Abraham, and the GOD of Isaac, and the GOD of Jacob" (Matthew 22:31-32, Acts 3:12-13, Exodus 3:4- 6, Exodus 3:15).

GOD is the "I AM THAT I AM" (Exodus 3:14).

Now, according to the word of GOD, even Galatians 3:16, John 3:16 - would you allow GOD to be your Father?

Have you decided to give your life over to Jesus Christ?

If yes, prayerfully say: - *Lord Jesus Christ, I am sure you see my heart and life, have mercy on me, from this moment; I take you as my Lord and Savior, I believe in you, connect me to your Father in your name I pray, Amen.*

This book is live by GOD's grace and so you may contact for more prayer and counseling.

The next chapter, by GOD's grace gives insight from GOD's Word as to what is next after this world is passed away.

CHAPTER 6: REAL WORD

Old Heaven and Earth

" And no one puts new wine into old wineskins; or else the new wine will burst the wineskins and be spilled, and the wineskins will be ruined. "But new wine must be put into new wineskins, and both are preserved – Luke 5:37-38 NKJV.
(Also, Matthew 9:17, Mark 2:22).

A man is not in this world just to eat, drink and die. Man is entirely eternal bound (Jeremiah 29:4-14). Nothing is casual even if it may seem casual (Matthew 12:36).
The things done (deeds) even clothes worn are not casual (Romans 2:6).

…. For the things which are seen are temporary, but the things which are not seen are eternal – 2 Corinthians 4:18b NKJV

When he had called the multitude to himself, he said to them, "Hear and understand: Not what goes into the man defiles a man: but what comes out of the mouth, this defiles a man." – Matthew 15:10-11 NKJV also, Mark 7:15.

Invariably, anything or everything a man, consciously or unconsciously says and/or does, has a source from within him (Luke 17:21).

A man with absolutely no eyes (i.e. blind) and then he suddenly receives two brand new and good eyes (miracle) even physically, is not a casual occurrence. It shows that man is not just Earthly but also eternally bound.

There is GOD (Psalms chapter 14).

The fact that Science has it that "All enzymes are protein, but not all protein are enzymes", would help us understand that Scripture(s) gives us insight that all words are spirit (John 6:63, 1 Corinthians 5:3-4) but words alone may not be sufficient to be spirit.

The book of Mark chapter five from verse one to verse twenty, shows that unclean spirits came out of the mad man and entered into swine but the swine could not speak out (words) as a man nevertheless, the swine were possessed with the unclean (evil) spirits before they perished into the sea.

The only words that are sufficient to be spirit are the words that would never pass away after this Heaven and Earth is passed away. They are the words of Christ Jesus (John 6:63).

"Heaven and Earth will pass away, but My words will by no means pass away. – Matthew 24:35a NKJV.

It is only Jesus Christ that would never pass away therefore, any man that would not pass away with this world (Heaven and Earth), must give his life over to Jesus Christ.

However, that day and hour when the present Heaven and Earth would pass away, knows no man (Matthew 25:36).

This present Heaven and Earth, is passed away for a dead person.

At the second coming of Christ Jesus, this Heaven and Earth shall be passed away for all persons.

New Heaven and Earth

If a man that is in Christ Jesus passes on, he goes to be in paradise (Luke 23:43, Luke 16:22) until the second coming of Jesus Christ.

At the second coming of Christ Jesus, both them that are in paradise and them that are still in the world whose names are found in the book of life, shall come with him into a New Heaven and Earth (GOD's Kingdom) (Matthew 24:31, 1 Corinthians chapter 15, 1 Thessalonians 4:16-17, Revelation 21:1-7).

In other words, a new body would they assume (courtesy Christ Jesus [GOD]) as to be able to enter and stay in the new place.

On the other hand, if a man is not in Christ Jesus or his name not found by the Holy angels in the book of life before he passes on, such a one goes to hell (hades) (Luke 16:19-23 until the second coming of Jesus Christ.
[May hell never be your portion in Jesus Christ name].

At Christ second coming, both them in hell and them that are still in the world whose names are not found in the book of life, shall be cast into the lake of fire (hell-fire) together with Satan and his cohort (Revelation 20:7-15). In other words, in their new body or form, they would enter and stay in their new place of everlasting torment (Mark 9:43-48, Isaiah 51:7-8).

Receive the power of GOD for everlasting life in Jesus Christ name! (Romans 10:1-17).

In accordance to Luke 5:37-38;

..................….......………………………….

Old Heaven and Earth – Man is as the old wine,

This world is as the old wine skin.

After the second coming of Christ Jesus

New Heaven and Earth – Man in new body is as the new wine,

GOD's kingdom to saints is as the new wine skin.

Lake of fire to sinners is as their new wine skin.

(See 2 Corinthians 5:1-21).

………………………………………….

Now I saw a new heaven and a new earth, for the first heaven and the first earth had passed away. Also, there was no more sea. Then I, John, saw the holy city, New Jerusalem, coming down out of heaven from GOD, prepared as a bride adorned for her husband. And I heard a loud voice from heaven saying, "Behold, the tabernacle of GOD is with men, and He will dwell with them, and they shall be His people. GOD Himself will be with them and be their GOD. And God will wipe away every tear from their eyes; there shall be no more death, nor sorrow, nor crying. There shall be no more pain, for the former things have passed away."

Then he who sat on the throne said, "Behold I make all things new." And He said to me, "Write, for these words are true and faithful". And He said to me, "It is done!

I am the Alpha and the Omega, the Beginning and the End. I will give of the fountain of the water of life freely too him who thirsts.

He who overcomes shall inherit all things, and I will be his GOD and he shall be My son. But the cowardly, unbelieving, abominable, murderers, sexually immoral, sorcerers, idolater and all liars shall have their part in the lake which burns with fire and brimstone, which is the second death" – Revelation 21:1-19 NKJV also, Revelation chapter 21.

But we speak the wisdom of GOD in a mystery, the hidden wisdom which GOD ordained before the ages for our glory, which none of the rulers of this age knew; for had they known, they would not have crucified the Lord of glory. But as it is written: "Eye has not seen, nor ear heard, nor have entered into the heart of man the things which God has prepared for those who love him." But God has revealed them to us through His spirit. For the Spirit searches all things, yea, the deep things of God. – 1 Corinthians 2:7- 10 NKJV.

GOD makes his sun to rise on both the evil and on the good in this world; He sends rain on the just and on the unjust (Matthew 5:45).

In the New Heaven and Earth to come, the Light of GOD will only shine on the good; rain only on the just (Revelation 22:3-5, Zechariah 14:17, Isaiah 60:19).

In this world, God hath mercy on whomever He wills (Romans 9:18).

In the New Heaven and Earth to come, the mercy of GOD will only be on those found in Jesus Christ (Zephaniah 2:3, Matthew 5:7).

In this world and forever, Jesus Christ is the goodness, righteousness and mercy of GOD to those that believe in Him (Philippians 4:13).

At his return, heirs of GOD's Kingdom shall never have evil birds/mentality flying over them, for those thought(s)/temptation would be totally removed from them forever (Zephaniah 3:9-13).
Halleluiah!

CHAPTER 7: SPIRITUAL WARFARE

At-a-Stretch (One)

SIN - expecting a definition -?
See 1 John 3:4.

Jesus Christ may not necessarily have to list sins of every individual he encounters nevertheless, He said it all.
In darkness, when light sets in, the darkness might not understand the light but darkness knows in a context that there is a difference.

In other words, dark kingdom of the spiritual realm knows Jesus Christ whenever they encounter him which is enough conviction to set free, man's spirit.

...and the evil spirit answered and said, Jesus I know – Acts 19:15a KJV.

Every human being is a spirit being and could either attach himself to the kingdom of GOD or to the Kingdom of darkness (Romans 8:16-17, John 8:42-44, Matthew 6:24).

John the Baptist who prepared the way, emphatically dealt with the issue of sin in the life of man even towards Herod (Matthew 14:1-4).

John the Apostle also did with further details as to the sin that leads to death and sin that is not unto death (1 John 5:16-19).
According to him, believers in Christ know that they are dead to Sin and dead works, by Grace (1 John 1:4-6, 1 John 3:10).

Therefore, see more into sin that does not lead to death as there are realms of godliness that may not be reached now just because of human nature in this world (Luke 3:22).
Notwithstanding, as much as Grace helps, a man should do away with such obstacles or realms that does not utterly please GOD.

....If we say that we have no sin, we deceive ourselves, and the truth is not in us – 1 John 1:8-9 KJV

...Whatsoever things are honest, whatsoever things are just... think on these things – Philippians 4:8 KJV.

A question was asked that can a Christian sin?

Answer --- 'Can' is a problem and might cause all the problems; as though a man has been instructed or mandated to sin. Apostle Paul gave insight about the mandate of a Christian in Hebrews 6:1-9.

Therefore, saints understand at least because the DNA (blood system) of the Heavenly Father flows in and through them.
A man caught up in grace would automatically not break the law simply because grace is a spiritual realm higher, easier and more interesting than the spiritual realm of the law, which is made manifest (Romans chapter 1 – chapter 6).

To be caught up in GOD's grace, someone must surrender his or her life unto Jesus Christ (John 15:4) so as not to break GOD's law.
GOD's law is beyond the one (1) instruction (Genesis 2:15-17), the ten (10) commandment (Exodus chapter 20) or the one hundred plus (100+) instruction (Leviticus chapter 1 - chapter 27).

Jesus the Christ, knows and understand all the law of GOD.

But this shall be the covenant that I will make with the house of Israel after those days, saith the LORD, I will put my law in their inward parts, and write it in their hearts; and will be their GOD, and they shall be my people - Jeremiah 31:33 NKJV also, Hebrews 10:14-17.

Once a man is in Christ and Christ in him, he is covered and would not just break GOD's law (1 John 3:6) rather he enjoys GOD, come what may. (2 Corinthians 4:17-18).

At-a-Stretch (Two)

SALVATION – expecting a definition -?
See John chapter 3, Acts 4:12.

An adage says – 'like father, like son'. It means that a son does like his father. A child of GOD act, does, think and behave like his Heavenly Father (GOD) under the canopy of born again (under Jesus).

The ultimate salvation is eternal life.

And I give unto them eternal life; and they shall never perish, neither shall any man pluck them out of my hand. – John 10:28 KJV.

It is good that a man (male or female) have a good life on Earth. *I am come that they might have life, - John 10:10b* nevertheless, it is ultimately good that a man has life eternal (in abundance) ... *and that they might have it more abundantly. – John 10:10c.*

In other words, to break away from Earthly curses is good however, away from eternal curses is the ultimate goal.

Beloved, I wish above all things that thou mayest prosper and be in health, even as thy soul prospereth – 3 John 2 KJV.

Why is Salvation of a Personal Decision?

The word of the LORD came to me again, saying, "What do you mean when you use this proverb concerning the land of Israel, saying: 'The fathers have eaten sour grapes, And the Children's teeth are set on edge'?"
"As I live," says the Lord GOD, "you shall no longer use this proverb in Israel. "Behold, all souls are mine; The soul of the father as well as the soul of the Son is Mine; The soul who sins shall die – Ezekiel 18:1-4 NKJV

The word of the LORD came again to me, saying: "Son of man, when a land sins against Me by persistent unfaithfulness, I will stretch out My hand against it; I will cut off its supply of bread, send famine on it, and cut off man and beast from it. Even if these three men, Noah, Daniel and Job, were in it, they would deliver only themselves by their righteousness," says the Lord GOD. "If I cause wild beasts to pass through the land, and they empty it and make it so desolate that man may pass through because of the beasts, even though these three men were in it, as I live," says the Lord GOD, "they would deliver neither sons nor daughters; only they would be delivered, and the land would be desolate. – Ezekiel 14:12-16 NKJV

Therefore no one would be declared righteous in GOD's sight by the works of the law; rather through the law we become conscious of our sin. But now apart from the law, the righteousness of GOD has been made known, to which the Law and the Prophets testify. This righteousness is given through faith in Jesus Christ to all who believe. There is no difference between Jew and Gentile for all have sinned and fall short of the glory of GOD and all are justified freely by his grace through the redemption that came by Christ Jesus. GOD presented Christ as a sacrifice of atonement, through the shedding of his blood – to be received by faith. He did this to demonstrate his righteousness, because in his forbearance he had left the sins committed beforehand unpunished – he did it to demonstrate his righteousness at the present time, so as to be just and the one who justifies those who have faith in Jesus. Where, then is boasting? It is excluded. Because of what law? The law that requires works? No, because of the law that requires faith. For we maintain that a person is justified by faith apart from the works of the law. Or is GOD the GOD of Jews only? Is he not the GOD of Gentiles too? Yes, of Gentiles too, since there is only one

GOD, who will justify the circumcised by faith and the uncircumcised through that same faith. Do we, then, nullify the law by this faith?
Not at all! Rather, we uphold the law –
Romans 3:20-31 NIV

Armageddon

End-time battle (Revelation chapter 16 also, Matthew chapter 24, Daniel chapter 2, Daniel chapter 7, Daniel chapter 8, Daniel chapter 12).

The toughest attack on the end-time church is not only from the dreadful unbelievers of Christ Jesus such as magicians, sorcerers, witches and occultist ones, 'Herod' (Revelation 6:2-5) but it is also from the so called 'believers' that are Satanic; such as anti-Christ, false Pharisees, false Prophets, false Teachers (Fake white ones) (2 Thessalonians chapter 2, 1 John chapter 4, Jeremiah 44:15-18, 2 Peter 2:1-3).

The greatest battle ever fought and that would ever be fought in the history of mankind is not of blood-and-sand but of hell against Heaven. It is the on-going battle until Jesus Christ finally returns (second time) to authenticate the victory that He had already guaranteed.

In other words, it is the battle that saints of GOD are engaged in against 'sin', "Satan" and 'death'.

If, in the manner of men, I have fought with beasts at Ephesus, what advantage is it to me? If the dead do not rise, "Let us eat and drink, for tomorrow we die!"
Do not be deceived: "Evil Company corrupts good habits". Awake to righteousness, and do not sin; for some do not have the knowledge of GOD. I speak this to your shame. – 1 Corinthians 15:32-34 NKJV. Also, Hebrews 9:28.

For since by man came death, by Man also came the resurrection of the dead. For as in Adam all die, even so in Christ all shall be made alive. But each one in his own order: Christ the first fruits, afterward those who are Christ at His coming.

Then comes the end, when He delivers the kingdom to GOD the Father, when He puts an end to all rule and all authority and power. For He must reign till He has put all enemies under His feet. The last enemy that will be destroyed is death. – 1 Corinthians 15:21-26 NKJV.

It is by the blood of Jesus Christ, that a sinner becomes a saint (Hebrews 9:22).

The battle ground of Spiritual Warfare for a man is the heart/mind of that Man (Acts 14:2, Matthew 24:48, Ephesians 6:12, Galatians 5:26, Colossians 3:1-2, Matthew 16:23).

A perfect man or child of GOD, offends not in word (James 3:2, Proverbs 21:23, Ephesians 4:29, John 6:63, Matthew 5:48, James chapter 1).

In spiritual world; Number(s) One, Two, Three, Four, Five, Six and Seven might mean power, realm, day...

Number-One by the scriptures, is of perfection (Mark 10:6-9 also, Deuteronomy 6:4, Colossians 3:14, Revelation 19:9).

Number-Seven is also of perfection [such as assigned by GOD] (Genesis 2:2-4).

Number-Six is almost perfect but not perfect (Malachi chapter 2).

Therefore, Number-Six is not acceptable to GOD even the number (666) which is the mark of the beast (Revelation 13:16-18).

Number-Six seems higher and more powerful than Number(s) Five, Four, Three, Two and even One but Number-Six is same as Zero (0) to God because it is imperfection (almost perfect but not perfect).

Perfection (Jesus Christ) is the standard of GOD (Revelation chapter 21- chapter 22).

Powers or Forces operating as Number-Six, might be powerful enough to send down fire from above but it is not acceptable to GOD.

And I saw the beast, the Kings of the Earth, and their armies, gathered together to make war against Him who sat on the horse and against His army. Then the beast was captured, and with him the false Prophet who worked signs in his presence, by which they deceived those who received the mark of the beast and those who worshipped his image. These two were cast alive into the lake of fire burning with brimstone. – Revelation 19:19-20 NKJV. Also, Revelation 13:11-13.

It is only the fire of GOD that is acceptable by Him (Revelation 20:9).

No man (male or female) can truly meet up Godly standard and absolutely please GOD except Jesus Christ. Only through Jesus Christ can any man truly meet up Godly Standard/Perfection.

A standard not to be quantified by men but by GOD (Romans 3:3-4, Matthew 3:17, Hebrews 7:22, Romans 3:21-22, 1 Timothy 2:5).

The world is constantly in tumult whether of natural disaster, human disaster and so on, majorly because of her sin against GOD [Book of Nahum].

More wickedness is done even the more in these times not often by bows and arrows but by the Craftiness and Mischievousness in/from the heart of men (Luke 22:53, Matthew 24:12, Ecclesiastes 7:29).

There is one accuser, oppressor, deceiver [Satan] (John 10:10, 1 Corinthians 15:56-57).

The power to live above sin is in Christ Jesus!

Be not deceived that anti-Christ comes with a special name, figure or at a stipulated date from this time. It is already here. Anything that is against Christ is anti- Christ; not just of words alone but also of deeds. BEWARE! (1 John 2:18).

Full-time is expired, it is now times of extra-time (Revelation 20:6-9, Daniel 12:7, Revelation 12:14).

In Football, extra-time requires extra energy, effort, wisdom, targeted goals, breath, team work…
In this world, extra-time requires extra of GOD's oil, love, joy, peace, temperance… for a child of GOD (Matthew 25:1-13, Galatians 5:16-26).

The salvation of any man that accepts Jesus Christ (whether he is alive now or sleeps), is finally sealed or authenticated when he (Jesus Christ) returns (Revelation 20:6, also Daniel 2:31-46).

He shall appear again in the air not to deal with sin anymore but to grant judgment to all. All eyes shall see him. Now, sins of men rob-off on him for their cleansing and purity because that is why he was slain as a lamb.

GOD has raised him from the dead and he is at the right hand of GOD now. He shall return at an hour when no one knoweth and as lion of the house of Judah; not to be killed but to devour his prey and save his own ones.

For the earnest expectation of the creature waiteth for the manifestation of the sons of GOD. – Romans 8:19 KJV.

(Matthew 24:30, Acts 17:31, Acts 1:11, Acts 3:19-21, 1 Corinthians chapter 3, 1 Corinthians chapter 15, John 1:29, Revelation 5:1-5, Hebrews 9:28, Jude, 1 and 2 Thessalonians, The book of Revelation).

The True white One (Jesus Christ), is the perfect One (such as assigned by GOD). He is greater than the fake white ones (Matthew 7:15, Revelation 1:12-20, Ephesians 1:21, Revelation 19:11-16).

TO THE KINGDOM OF GOD: The dead in Christ shall be in rise first, then those alive in Christ shall immediately join them (1Thessalonians 4:16-18).

TO HELL-FIRE: The false Prophet(s) and the evil beast would be in fall, in the bottomless pit, then the devil shall be cast there (Revelation 20:10, Revelation 9:2).
Yet all these things shall happen in the twinkling of an eye (twinkling of human eye) (1Corinthians 15:45-57).

For the time has come for judgment to begin at the house of God; and if it begins with us first, what will be the end of those who do not obey the gospel of God?

Now "If the righteous one is scarcely saved, where will the ungodly and the sinner appear?" – 1 Peter 4:17-18 NKJV.

Therefore, **repent** for the kingdom of GOD is at hand! (Matthew 4:17, John 10:25-30).

Revelation chapter 20 gives spiritual insight into the mystery of – "A thousand years (Millennial reign)".

At first resurrection (first rapture); born again ones are dead to sin and raised alive in Christ, even seated with him in heavenly places (Ephesians 2:4-7) despite that they are still in this world as natural men and women or even if they sleep (This is the essence of water baptism ever since the days of John the Baptist and this is salvation experience – Matthew 11:12, Romans 10:9- 10).

Nevertheless, after a time as assigned by GOD (a very short time) of the whole creational history; which is not a timing quantified or known by men, Christ Jesus shall return for judgment and children of God shall be resurrected by him and to him forever (second resurrection or rapture).

Blessed and holy is he who has part in the first resurrection. Over such the second death has no power, but they shall be priests of God and of Christ, and shall reign with Him a thousand years. – Revelation 20:6 NKJV

In other words, from Revelation 20:6c to Revelation 20:15 with excerpts from Ezekiel chapter 38 and 39, Daniel chapter 8; explains what would happen at the interval of the first and second resurrection.

The second resurrection shall be the sort out of names of those written in the book of life and otherwise; it shall happen in the twinkling of an eye (1 Corinthians 5:52) when Christ returns.

The millennial reign for a child of GOD is also a period where the kingdom of darkness reigns for the unsaved ones (Luke 22:53) of which in this world, it would be as though the kingdom of darkness reigns supreme (Luke 21:20, Revelation 20:7-9).

At the return of Christ, he and his saints shall reign supreme forever (when all things are made new) (Psalms 2:9, Revelation 2:25-29).

And no wonder! For Satan himself transforms himself into an angel of light. – 2 Corinthians 11:14 NKJV.

"And they overcame him by the blood of the Lamb and by the word of their testimony, and they did not love their lives to the death. – Revelation 12:11 NKJV.

For God has not given us a spirit of fear, but of power and of love and of a sound mind. – 2 Timothy 1:7 NKJV.

So shall they fear The name of the LORD from the west, And His glory from the rising of the sun; When the enemy comes in like a flood, The Spirit of the LORD will lift up a standard against him. – Isaiah 59:19 NKJV.

Keep your heart with all diligence, For out of it spring the issues of life. Put away from you a deceitful mouth, And put preserve lips far from you. – Proverbs 4:23-24 NKJV.

And do not be conformed to this world, but be transformed by the renewing of your mind, that you may prove what is that good and acceptable and perfect will of GOD. – Romans 12: 2 NKJV.

Looking unto Jesus, the author and finisher of our faith, who for the joy that was set before Him endured the cross, despising the shame, and has sat down at the right hand of the throne of GOD. – Hebrews 12:2 NKJV.

"He who has an ear, let him hear what the Spirit says to the churches. He who overcome shall not be hurt by the second death". – Revelation 2:11 NKJV.

Now may the God of peace Himself sanctify you completely; and may your whole spirit, soul and body be preserved blameless at the coming of our Lord Jesus Christ. –   1 Thessalonians 5:23 NKJV.

Please remember to highly rate and drop your honest review of this book on the site of purchase.

Thank you!

www.ingramcontent.com/pod-product-compliance
Lightning Source LLC
LaVergne TN
LVHW051954060526
838201LV00059B/3650